Pain's Hidden Purpose

Pain's Hidden Purpose

Finding Perspective in the Midst of Suffering

by
Don Baker

MULTNOMAH PRESS
PORTLAND, OREGON 97266

Unless otherwise indicated, all Scripture quotations are from the New American Standard Bible, © 1960, 1962, 1963, 1968, 1971, 1972, 1973, 1975, 1977 by The Lockman Foundation, La Habra, California. Used by permission.

Verses marked TLB are taken from The Living Bible, copyright 1971 by Tyndale House Publishers, Wheaton, Ill. Used by permission.

Cover design by Tom Williams

PAIN'S HIDDEN PURPOSE
© 1984 by Don Baker
Published by Multnomah Press
Portland, Oregon 97266

Printed in the United States of America

Library of Congress Cataloging in Publication Data

Baker, Don.
    Pain's hidden purpose.

    Bibliography: p. 111.
    1. Suffering—Biblical teaching.   2. Bible. O.T. Job—Criticism, interpretation, etc.   I. Title.
BS1199.S8B34   1983   231'.8   83-22135
ISBN 0-88070-035-1 (pbk.)

87 88 89 90 91 92 93 94 95 – 10 9 8 7 6 5 4 3 2

Table of Contents

**The story of Job
is the story of a man
who suffers
without a reason
and loses
without a cause—
and survives.**

Preface

I've never seen a man whose blackened and crusty body was covered with massive, draining sores, rocking back and forth in the ashes of a garbage dump. I've never heard the unending wailing or watched as the person scraped the crusted scabs from his body.

I've never known a man who lost all his wealth, possessions, and children in just one day.

I've seen other kinds of derelicts
   along the skid row
      under the bridges
         beside the railroad tracks.

I've seen them scavenging garbage cans, struggling against restraints in mental institutions, wasting away in hospital beds, or begging in their poverty.

I've seen the rich become poor—
I've seen the strong become weak—
I've watched the mighty fall and shatter like Humpty-Dumpties.

But I've never witnessed a spectacle quite like that of a man from Uz whose name was Job.[1]

Job's story is a real-life, time and space biographical sketch.

It's not a myth, a fantasy, or a legend. Simply because it's old doesn't mean it's not contemporary. It's as up-to-date as today.

It's the story of a man who lost everything.

It's not just a theological treatise. Although it is filled with theology. More time has been spent discussing the philosophical and theological implications of Job than any other book of the Bible.

One of my favorite Peanuts cartoons shows Charlie Brown in his favorite role—that of pitcher for his sandlot baseball team.

In the first cartoon frame we see him on the pitcher's mound in deep trouble. He looks toward the team at bat and exclaims, "Nine runs in a row—good grief!"

Then he opens his mouth and begins to wail, "What can I do?"

Schroeder walks out to the mound, dressed in his catcher's mask and chest protector, as Charlie Brown says, "We're getting slaughtered again, Schroeder . . . I don't know what to do . . .

"Why do we have to suffer like this?"

Schroeder just stands there and very philosophically answers:

"Man is born to suffer as the sparks fly upward."

Charlie Brown looks puzzled and says, "What did you say, Schroeder?"

Then Linus comes up from behind and says, "He's quoting from the Book of Job, Charlie Brown . . . seventh verse, fifth chapter." Linus continues with, "Actually, the problem of suffering is a very profound one, and . . ."

Before he can get another word out of his mouth, he is interrupted as Lucy chimes in. ". . . If a person has bad luck, it's because he's done something wrong, that's what I always say!!!"

Schroeder moves back into the little cluster of people surrounding Charlie Brown.

"That's what Job's friends told him, but I doubt it . . ."

Again Schroeder is interrupted by Lucy, who shouts, "What about Job's wife? I don't think she gets enough credit."

Schroeder continues: "I think a person who never suffers, never matures. . . . Suffering is actually very important . . ."

Lucy interrupts again and screams, "Who wants to suffer? Don't be ridiculous!!!"

By this time the whole team is gathered around Charlie Brown, including a wide-eyed Snoopy, who is listening to every word.

One player says, "But pain is a part of life, and . . ."

Another interrupts and says, "A person who speaks only of the patience of Job reveals that he knows very little of the book! Now the way I see it . . ."

Disgustedly Charlie Brown walks back to the pitcher's mound, looks at his ball team, one by one, and says, "I don't have a baseball team—I have a theological seminary!"[2]

The Book of Job is not just a theological treatise:

> It does show God at His best, and
> it does show Satan at his worst.
> It is a revelation of God's sovereignty, and
> it is a revelation of man's helplessness.

> But . . . it is first and foremost
>   the story of a real man,
>   living in a real country,
>   suffering a real calamity.

> It's the story of
>   one man's wealth
>   one man's family
>   one man's health
>   one man's reputation, and
>   one man's spirit

that is lost, destroyed, broken, and crushed beneath an intolerable load of pain and suffering.

> It's the story of
>   one man's God
>   one man's faith
>   one man's enemy
>   one man's friends, and
>   one man's bewilderment,

as all the traditional values and traditional roles are thrown out of focus.

It's the story of a man who suffers without a cause and loses without a reason—and survives.

It's different from most personal tragedies, however. It's one of the few that tells the whole story, unlike an autobiography where a person tells his own story—as he sees it; or a biography, where a person tells another's story—as he sees it. This story adds another dimension. It's the story of a man's life as he saw it and as others saw it, but it's the story as Satan and God saw it also. It's the whole story.

It addresses the ofttimes unanswerables, like:

> How did it happen?
>   and
> Why did it happen?

It's one man's story, but it's every man's story, for in Job we have the "full picture" of calamity and suffering. And the "full picture" of Job's calamity and suffering is the "full picture" of your sufferings and mine.

Don Baker

Part 1

LOOKING AT SUFFERING

———————

Little did Job realize
that, after the loss
of his wealth
and the death of his
children,
a new pain would
replace the old,
and the new pain
would be so intense that
even the loss of his
children
would be forgotten.

———————

Chapter One

Death–Disease–
Desertion

Job slept fitfully during that endless night following the burial of his ten children. The images of each of his seven wonderful sons and three beautiful daughters constantly filtered through a tortured memory. He saw their faces, heard their voices, listened to their laughter, recalled their words, and painfully remembered each of those cherished moments that began on the days they were born.

Seven sons and three daughters really doesn't say much, and yet that's all that's recorded for us in the opening chapters of Job's chronicle of tragedy. It reminds me of the brief, cryptic, sterile obituary notices one reads in a newspaper, or the meaningless list of facts that a minister might recall during a funeral service.

"Seven sons and three daughters"—such a statement of fact is grossly inadequate in describing the joy, the warmth, the oneness of a close-knit family that shared every meaningful moment of their lives together.

But now they were dead—all of them in one day. In one shattering moment ten vibrant, happy, hopeful, promising lives ceased to be—and Job's world ended.

There was no release from the grief that held his smitten soul in bondage. Job and his wife found no comfort in themselves or in each other. The sorrow that gripped them refused to let go.

Yesterday was a nightmare. Today promised to be no better.

As the morning light first appeared over the mountains of the east, Job must have thought that no man anywhere had ever suffered such pain and such loss. No man anywhere could ever experience anything worse.

Little did he know what God was about to allow. Little did he realize that his own suffering had just begun. Little did he know that before this new day ended, a new pain would replace the old, and the new pain would be so intense that even the loss of his children would be forgotten.

The new pain began with an itch. As Job awoke from restless sleep he soon became aware that his body was inflamed with a sore and angry swelling. The red spots that covered his flesh were hot and tender to the touch.

They spread quickly over his entire body until he was covered with one universal boil that stretched from his head to his feet.

> His bones ached.
> His legs began to thicken.
> His hair fell out.
> His face swelled, and
> his voice became hoarse.

His entire appearance changed until his face became grim and distorted. His skin was encrusted and constantly running with pus. (See Albert Barnes, *Job,* vol. 1 [Grand Rapids: Baker Book House, 1949], p. 116).

To simply state that Job was smitten with sore boils from head to foot[1] does not begin to explain the extent of his sufferings. To add the words, "he scraped himself with a piece of broken pottery,"[2] suggests more, but still not enough.

To state that due to the chronic and contagious nature of his disease and the hideousness of his appearance, he was banished to the local garbage dump to sit in the ashes,[3] suggests the ultimate isolation but still fails to say it all.

Job describes the enormity of his immense and interminable suffering by stating that—

> He could not sleep—he continually tossed until dawn.[4]
> He used dirt clods to cover his running sores.[5]

Worms crawled in his flesh.[6]
The thought of food made him sick.[7]
His pain was so intense that he was forced to bite his
    own flesh to tear out the boils.[8]
His flesh rotted before his very eyes.[9]
The itching never ceased.[10]

He was flushed and red from weeping.
His eyes were dark and recessed from lack of sleep.[11]
His body was shriveled and wrinkled.[12]

Job was exhausted and alone.[13]
His breath was foul.[14]
He could barely breathe.[15]
His soul was bathed in bitterness.[16]

He was emaciated to the point that his bones clung to
    his skin.[17]
His flesh turned black.[18]
He was constantly burning with fever.[19]
And the pain never ceased.[20]

The only place he could find to rest was in the ashes
    and dung and garbage outside the city among
        the beggars
            the outcasts
                the lepers and
                    the dogs.
He was deserted by his friends and mocked by his
    enemies.[21]
He describes himself as a rag doll, grabbed by the neck
    and shaken to pieces.[22]
He was as a target set up and shot through with
    arrows.[23]

His condition was so desperate,
    his appearance so contemptible,
        his pain so continual,
            his shame so complete,
    that his wife finally suggested that he kill himself.

**Job, the most honored
man in the East,
began experiencing
a long,
uninterrupted series
of calamities
that led him
to the very brink
of self-destruction.**

Chapter Two

Even the Godly Suffer

Job's calamity had been sudden and complete. Just a few days before, one could find Job walking from his house each morning, along the sandswept streets of the Eastern city of Uz to its outer gate.[1] There he spent the day with his friends.

Job was an honored judge[2] in his hometown—noted for his fairness,[3] his integrity,[4] his compassion,[5] and his strong and compelling sense of justice.[6]

The young men of the city of Uz deferred to him, and the old ones stood in his honor whenever he entered the room.[7]

His advice was sought by all. Everyone listened when he spoke[8]—in fact it was generally agreed by all in Uz that when Job spoke, there was nothing more to be said.[9]

Everyone spoke well of Job.[10]

The widows in their loneliness were clothed and fed by his generosity.[11]

The blind often felt the gentle touch of his strong hands as he led them in their darkness.[12]

The lame were never left to their helplessness when Job was present.[13]

Even the strangers were welcomed by the greatness of this gracious gentleman.[14]

On numerous occasions Job received the Man-of-the-Year award in the city of Uz.[15]

His personality exuded a strength that even lightened the spirits of the discouraged.[16]

With firmness he corrected those in error—with wisdom he instructed the confused, and with great compassion he comforted those who mourned.[17]

There was no man on all the earth like Job.[18]

He was a man of immense wealth. His was the largest spread in all the East.[19] In a day when a man's wealth was measured by the size of his family, the size of his herds, the size of his flocks, the size of his staff, and the greatness of his reputation, Job exceeded them all.

It is said that everything he touched turned to gold—that even the rocks poured out streams of olive oil to him.[20]

He had a family that was unusually close—they did everything together—even after they were grown, married, and had left home.

They loved birthday parties. Whenever any one of the ten children had a birthday, it was a total family affair.

The sons and daughters with their children would gather together in one of their homes to celebrate. Sometimes these celebrations would last for as long as a week.[21]

Job was a good father, and as a good father in a patriarchal system, he was also a good priest to his family—long before the world knew anything of an official priesthood.

After each of the family birthday parties, Job would go over to his own little worship center and offer a special sacrifice to Jehovah God, just in case one of his children had said or done something that was offensive to God.[22]

The friendship of God was constantly felt in his home.[23]

There was no hint of discord among his children—no foolish talk of divorce or remarriage—no restlessness among his servants—just prosperity and peace—the longing of all—to be full and to be happy.

Job not only enjoyed a good reputation among his peers but, of even greater importance, he had a good reputation with God. God lovingly spoke of Job as one-of-a-kind, the only one like him on earth—one who was genuine and honest and without blame. Job had a vital, satisfying, and personal relationship that was above and beyond anyone in his generation.[24]

It was a beautiful picture of one man's family, one man's wealth, one man's God, delightfully situated in one man's community where this one man, Job, had all that a person could ever need—and more. He had all that a person could ever want.

Job felt the joy of the immense security that was his and even noted later that he honestly believed he would someday die quietly in his own little nest after a long and good life.[25]

And then, swiftly and without warning, tragedy struck, and all of Job's joy turned sour. Job's life changed, Job's world changed, and Job began experiencing a long, uninterrupted series of calamities that led him to the very brink of self-destruction.

**Job was slowly,
methodically,
being stripped to the
very nakedness of his
spiritual being.**

Chapter Three

Joy Turned Sour

Job lost it all—in just one day.

It was during one of those happy family celebrations that disaster struck.

All of the children were gathered in Job's eldest son's house, celebrating a birthday,[1] when Job received word from one of his servants that a group of terrorists from the south had suddenly and without warning plundered his herds and slain one of his work crews. Five hundred oxen and five hundred valuable female donkeys were gone, and all but one of his farm hands had been slain.[2]

At the same time that the sole survivor of the massacre was breathlessly describing the horrible event, another servant appeared and described the destruction of Job's 7,000 sheep and all but one of his shepherds.

"It was lightning," he said. "The fire of God fell down and burned the sheep and the servants and consumed them."[3]

"The camels are gone," shouted another. "All 3000 of them."

Those wonderful beasts of burden, invaluable to the desert community, were gone, stolen by another group of terrorists—this time from the north. Again, all but one of his servants were slain—and all of this in one day—his son's birthday.[4]

Suddenly, the rich man had become poor.

> His stock market had collapsed.
> His business had failed.
> His creditors had foreclosed.
> His lenders had refused to extend his line of credit.
> He had lost his job.

However we might wish to describe it, Job had lost it all.
The richest man in the East was broke.

It was probably at this time that Job turned to his wife and said, "Well, Honey, we may have lost all of our herds and all of our flocks and most of our servants, but at least we have our family."

Without warning, tragedy struck again. Another messenger appeared, bearing the worst news a parent can hear—

"Your children are dead, all of them. They were celebrating your son's birthday when a tornado struck. The whole house collapsed and fell in on them, and all of the young people are dead."[5]

There is no easy way to share that devastating news with a parent. I have been forced to do it many times. I've tried to find just the right series of words and phrases appropriately designed to soften the blow, but with no success. Those words fall with the force of a hammer on the tender heart of an unsuspecting parent, and something fragile is crushed forever.

Job was devastated. In great grief he ripped his robe from his body, shaved the hair from his head to tell the world that all his glory was gone, then fell to the ground and sobbed.[6]

I've often wondered just how long it took for those sobs to subside before he called out to God. And I've wondered if the recorded words were his first ones.[7]

Although the Scriptures say Job did not sin or revile against God with his lips,[8] I'm sure he did question, and like all of us, as he lay there on the ground sobbing in his grief, I'm sure he asked, "Why?" "Why?" "Why?"

Martha and I have stood on a wind-swept hillside, transfixed by the sight of a little white casket in which lay the lifeless form of our only child.

Occasionally the sun would break through the clouds and shine like a spotlight on that little wooden box. And then it would drift back into hiding, and the gray gloom of an early spring day would again fall down around us.

Friends were there
    family was there
        beloved pastor was there—

and yet we remember nothing but the awesome feelings of emptiness, as if all life, all joy, all hope, all laughter had been squeezed from our very souls—forever.

The memory of that little white casket silhouetted against the green hillside is just as vivid today, thirty years later, as it was on that May afternoon.

The pain has eased, and yet occasionally I'll catch sight of a single tear as it rolls down Martha's cheek, and I'll know that something has stirred the memory of a little life that was loaned to us for such a short time.

It hurts—deeply—to lose someone we love.

To multiply that loss by ten and to be forced to stand beside the caskets of seven sons and three daughters—all you have—is beyond comprehension.

Job's world had ended. Job's life was over.

All the plans for the future suddenly ceased to exist—there was no future—only a past. And even the memories of the past were now no longer pleasant, but haunting—as Job slowly, painfully watched his children, one by one, lowered out of sight, into the sand, beyond his reach—forever.

Job did manage to worship—without benefit of any divine manuscript or printed revelation. Long before even the words of Moses were transcribed, Job worshiped. And he worshiped Jehovah God—the same God worshiped by Adam and Noah and Abraham.

He didn't know much, but he knew enough to bow in

    simple,
        spontaneous,
            unstructured,
                genuine worship,

and say:

> "Naked I came from my mother's womb,
> And naked I shall return there.
> The Lord gave and the Lord has taken away.
> Blessed be the name of the Lord.[9]

These were profound words dropping from the lips of a man whose revelation of God was yet incomplete—and these were possibly premature words since the greater pain was yet to follow.

These worshipful phrases bore little resemblance to the words which flew outward and upward in response to the greater torment that wracked his body as he lay writhing in pain and torment among the garbage and ashes.

Many have speculated as to just what Job's wife may have meant when she looked at that emaciated and blackened body and suggested that he end his suffering.

Some see Job's wife at this point as hardened and bitter—unconcerned for his relationship with God. I see her as a sensitive, caring, concerned woman who loved Job and honored her commitment. No family could have enjoyed the oneness Job's family shared if their mother had been calloused or cruel.

But she was stretched. Weeks of suffering had passed without relief. Each morning she'd wake to the same pain, only to find it intensified. Each night she'd pray for her husband's healing, but it never came—and there was no medication—

> no Tylenol #3
>   no Percodan
>   no Demarol
>   no morphine to ease the pain
>   no Seconal
>   no Valium
>   not even aspirin to help him sleep.

His suffering was so intense, his looks so hideous, his condition so infectious that he was forced to move out.

She could stand it no longer. In a moment of deep and frustrated anguish she suggested, "Job, why don't you curse God and die?"

> "Tell God you've had enough."
> "He's not able to heal you."
> "He's gone back on His promise."
> "He's not even aware of your problem."
> "I'd rather see you dead than like this—"
> "Maybe we could die together."

Again, Job's response was profoundly worshipful—simple, yet filled with deep insights; he said, "Woman, you're talking like one of those foolish ones—one of those unbelievers. Shall we accept good from God and not accept adversity?"[10] And he rejected her suggestion.

Besides the physical pain, the emotional and spiritual anguish was immense.

He was a man with a broken body and a broken spirit.

Occasionally he'd have flashbacks to the good old days—"the years gone by,"[11] he called them—the days

> when God took care of him,[12]
> when God's friendship was felt in his home,[13]
> when all his children were around him,[14]
> when his life prospered,[15]
> when the elders honored him,[16] and
> the young men stepped aside and revered him,[17]
> when even the highest officials in the city stood in respect for him.[18]

But that was long ago—that's gone. In place of honor and prosperity, now—

> The young men made fun of him.[19]
> He was a joke to them.[20]
> They'd spit in his face.[21]
> They'd lay traps for his path.[22]
> They'd come at him from all directions.[23]
> He lived in terror—with no one to help.[24]
> Depression haunted his days.[25]
> He'd cry to God but get no answer.[26]
> His voice of joy and gladness had turned to mourning.[27]

Job's state was so horrible that even his wife finally deserted him.[28]

Job was slowly, methodically, being stripped to the very nakedness of his spiritual being.

All the things that clothe the spirit of man were being ripped from him.

All that man leans upon for help and strength was taken from him until all that was left was a soul that was forced to stand naked and alone in the universe of God.

"Job, you have sinned."

Chapter Four

Good Friends– Bad Counsel

Bad news travels fast. Eliphaz, Bildad, and Zophar, long-time friends of Job, soon heard of his dreadful condition. They made an appointment to meet in Uz.[1] They'd heard the rumors and listened to the stories, but they were totally unprepared for what they saw.

Job's great pastures were vacant—his servants' quarters empty—his house deserted. The shutters banged in the wind, the yard was overgrown, the magnificent ranch of the once-mighty Job, richest man in all of the East, was desolate.

Neighbors finally directed them to the local garbage dump.

At first they failed to recognize him.[2] His black, emaciated, pus-encrusted body, covered with ashes, bore no resemblance to that of the honored judge of the city of Uz.

With a startled cry they saw him. These three were so over-whelmed by the sight of Job's condition—

they screamed—
they tore their clothes—
they threw ashes over their heads—
then—they became silent.

For seven days and seven nights[3] they sat alongside this friend whose body now bore little resemblance to that of a human being.[4]

For seven days and seven nights they watched him writhing in pain.[5]

For seven days and seven nights they listened to his soul as it poured out unutterable words of torment.

For seven days and seven nights no one spoke.[6] They simply tried to comprehend the incomprehensible—to understand the magnitude of this tragedy—to answer, in their own minds, the one elusive, evasive, tormenting question—WHY?

Job could restrain himself no longer. After seven days of silence he said:[7]

> I wish God would erase my birthday from His calendar.
> I wish I had never been conceived.
> Why didn't I die at birth?
> Why didn't my mother have a miscarriage?
> Why can't I die now?
> If only I could rest in death.
> If only I could be at ease in the grave.
> If only I could be free from this slavery.
> Why has God done this to me?

Sixteen times Job hurled that word "why" into the heavens. Sixteen times it flew outwards and upwards. And each time he cried for an answer, the heavens were silent. But his friends were not.

Eliphaz, Bildad, and Zophar attempted to answer the unanswerable. That's always a mistake—at least it's always a mistake to answer that question with the air of finality displayed by Job's counselors.

Not only did they claim the ability to comprehend the incomprehensible, they did it with an alarming display of arrogance and with a complete absence of compassion.

Notice how these three "comforters" spoke to Job—

"Will you let me say a word," said Eliphaz.[8]

"In the past you have told many a troubled soul to trust in God and have encouraged those who are weak or falling, or lie crushed upon the ground or tempted to despair.

"But now, when trouble strikes, you faint and are broken."

Eliphaz heaped guilt on top of Job's pain.

Bildad began his speech by saying, "How long will you go on like this, Job, blowing words around like the wind?"[9]

Bildad piled criticism on top of Job's suffering.

Zophar interrupted by saying, "Shouldn't someone stem this torrent of words? Is a man proved right by all this talk?"[10]

Zophar stacked sarcasm on top of Job's agony.

The insensitivity of these three is awesome.

Their main premise, and their only premise, in these interminable arguments with Job was that Job's suffering was the result of his sin.

Eliphaz said, "Stop and think! Have you ever known a truly good and innocent person who was punished?"[11]

Bildad said, "If you were pure and good, God would hear your prayer and answer you and bless you with a happy home."[12]

Zophar said, "You claim you are pure in the eyes of God! Oh, that God would tell you what He thinks! Oh, that He would make you truly see yourself, for He knows everything you have done. Listen! God is doubtless punishing you far less than you deserve!"[13]

These three had but one message to give Job, and they repeated it over and over again. Their unchanging word was:

> "Job, you have sinned."
> "Your suffering is due to your sin."
> "Repent and be healed."

And Job's response never varied:[14]

> "I know the difference between right and wrong."
> "My one comfort is that I have not denied the words of God, and now, when you should be kind to a fainthearted friend, you have accused me without the slightest fear of God."
> "Tell me, what have I done wrong?"
> "O God, please tell me why You're doing this to me."[15]
> "Did You create me just for the purpose of destroying me?"

Finally their accusations became specific. They said:[16]

"Job, your sins are endless."
"You must have refused to loan money to needy friends unless they gave you all their clothing as a pledge."
    or
"You must have refused water to the thirsty and bread to the starving."
"You sent widows away without helping them, and broke the arms of orphans."

Job replied:[17]

"I have not looked with lust upon a girl."
"I have not lied."
"I have not longed for another man's wife."
"I have not been unfair to my servants."
"I have not hurt the widows or orphans"
    or
"refused food to the hungry"
    or
"harmed an enemy."
"I have never even turned away a stranger."
"Look," he says, "I'll even sign an affidavit claiming my innocence."
"But let Almighty God answer me and show me where I am wrong."

Nine times Job's friends called him into account for his sins.

Nine times they told him that he was suffering because he had sinned—and that his suffering continued because he refused to repent.

Nine times Job denied their accusations.

For twenty-eight chapters they engaged in a running argument that increased in volume to a virtual shouting match—

"You sinned," they said.
"I did not," Job answered.
"You did"
"I didn't"
"You did too"
"I did not"

until finally three would-be comforters, turned accusers, had nothing more to say.

Job sat still in his loneliness and in his pain, and Eliphaz, Bildad, and Zophar became quiet in their frustration and bewilderment. Nothing had been accomplished—

> no comfort delivered—
>   no pain relieved—
>   no insights gained.

Job still hurt, and his one dominant question, "Why?", still remained unanswered.

Pain speaks a strange
language—
it plays funny tricks
on us.
It makes us think and
say things
and even believe things
that are not true.

Chapter Five

The Strange Language
of Pain

Sitting quietly in the ashes was another—one who until now had been quiet and restrained. He was a shy young man[1] who hardly felt competent to become a part of the illustrious team of theological debaters. He had listened to every word. He had heard every argument—among them words that he personally felt lowered the dignity of Almighty God.

He didn't seem to be overly impressed with the long list of accusations and their vehement denials, but he was angry—angry that Job had continued to maintain his innocence when some of his statements bordered on blasphemy, and angry with his three friends because they had condemned Job without a reason.[2]

"I feel like a new wineskin that's about to burst," he began. "I can contain myself no longer. I must speak to get relief."[3] "Job, please listen to me. You are wrong in what you say about God."[4]

To be told that he was wrong was nothing new. That had been his friends' theme song for days. They had repeatedly told him he was wrong, but that was different. They had said over and over again that he was wrong in what he had said about himself—that he was wrong about his innocence. But Elihu was saying something totally different. Elihu was claiming that Job was saying something wrong about God.

Job was silent. He listened as Elihu listed the condemning statements that had fallen unthinkingly from Job's lips—statements common to all of us when we're submerged beneath the murky waters of pain.

Pain speaks a strange language—it plays funny tricks on us. It makes us think things and say things and even believe things that are not true. When pain begins to bore its way through human flesh and on into human spirit and then just sit there and hurt and hurt and hurt, the mind becomes clouded and the brain begins to think strange thoughts like—

> God is dead
> or
> He's gone fishing
> or
> He's just plain not interested.

In Job's attempt to find the cause of his suffering, he did what many of us do. He began lowering God from His position of uniqueness and began ascribing motives and thoughts that were more like man's than God's. He then proceeded to attack God verbally, with statements like:

> God is fighting me.[5]
> God is ignoring me.[6]
> I might as well have sinned.[7]

These statements are so human, aren't they? Many times I've heard God's people say, "It seems like God is just sitting up there inventing new ways to make my life miserable." Or,

"It seems like God has turned a deaf ear to me. He has directed His attention elsewhere. He has decided never to listen to my prayer again." Or,

"It seems like my whole life has taken a turn for the worse, since I became a Christian. I sometimes feel I would have been better off without Christ."

Job's complaints against God are not unique to the day in which he lived. I have heard them time and again. I have thought them. Yes, I have even spoken them myself.

In correcting the, would-be counselors, Elihu gave a brilliant defense for God (Who really needs no defense) but, at the same time, heaped new pain on the already overburdened Job.

He said to Job:[8]

> "You have spoken like a fool."
> "You should be given the maximum penalty for the wicked way you have talked to God."
> "For now you have added rebellion, arrogance, and blasphemy to your other sins."

And then again, "Job, you have spoken like a fool."[9]

I shall always be deeply grateful for a nonjudgmental counselor who loved me, listened to me, and tolerated me during the time of my deep depression. There were times I thought things, said things, and did things for which I justly deserved a rebuke.

My friend handled my very fragile spirit with the tenderest of care. He listened to my nonsense—nonsense that originated somewhere deep within my aching soul. He listened to my incoherence—incoherence that emanated from deep within a bewildered mind. He listened—and listened—and listened—and all the time he was listening, he refused to play God in my life.

He did not know why I was depressed, and he freely admitted it.

He fully expected irrational statements. He heard them and then let them fall—and he let them lie—without even dignifying them with a response.

Those who have ever hurt deeply know the value of a friend who, even though he may think he knows the answer, is willing just to listen to the questions.

Job's friends never really heard Job—oh, yes, they heard the words that dropped from his lips, but they were deaf to the cry of his soul. The one cry that kept coming from the heart of this man who had been completely stripped of all dignity was, "Why? Why is God doing this to me? What have I done? What have I done?" That question can never be answered by a man—or by a woman. Only God knows and only God knows just how much of the answer He can ever share with us.

In addition to his great pain, great guilt was heaped on him. And Job just sat there—in the ashes—in his torment—waiting. Waiting for deliverance—waiting for death—little realizing that he was really waiting for God who was just about to arrive.

**Explanations don't
heal people—
but they can certainly
change the complexion
of an illness.**

Chapter Six

God Appears

All Job wanted was an explanation. Even the severest pain becomes somewhat tolerable with knowledge.

Many years ago my father began suffering with severe back pain, a pain so intense that it not only affected him physically, but mentally. Unable to work, he became depressed and began to withdraw as doctor after doctor was unable to diagnose the cause of his illness.

I was with him in the hospital on the day they finally discovered the problem. He lay silent in his bed, face turned to the wall, unresponsive and detached.

The doctor called us out into the hall and told us that the problem was cancer—inoperable and terminal. Then he asked, "Should I tell your father?" We all agreed that Dad should know—and quickly.

We listened from outside the door as the doctor, with his best bedside manner, tried to say those terribly difficult words that all of us fear.

"Harry, can you hear me?"

"Yes," Dad answered.

"Harry, I'm sorry to tell you this, but you have cancer."

"Oh?"

"Yes," the doctor went on, "cancer of the prostate—it has spread throughout your whole body. It's in your bones, Harry."

"Will I get better, Doctor?" Dad asked.

"No, Harry."

"How long do I have?"

"Maybe a few weeks, maybe a few months, we don't know," the doctor said.

With those words, Dad pulled himself up on the bed, looked straight into the eyes of his doctor, and said, "Is that all that's wrong with me? Hand me my clothes, please. I've got lots of things to get done."

His pain was no less severe, but Dad went back home, went back to work, and with sheer determination lived for nearly three years, long enough to see me finish school and become pastor of my first church—a church in which he served as a deacon.

Explanations don't heal people—but they can certainly change the complexion of an illness.

An explanation was what Job was asking for—an opportunity to speak to God.[1]

> A showdown
>   a confrontation
>   a high-noon face-off

where he could demand from God a reason for his suffering.

Finally it happened. Elihu was speaking. He was paying a beautiful tribute to God—painting word pictures that described[2]

> God's righteousness and
>   God's knowledge and
>   God's justice.

He pleaded with Job[3] not to seek death and not to turn to evil and to remember that there are some things we just cannot know about God.

Elihu lifted his head and directed his words to the growing storm clouds.

> "Look how great God is—we don't begin to know Him or to understand Him. He draws up the water vapor and then distills it into rain, which the skies pour down."[4]

Elihu held out his hands to catch the first of the falling rain drops.

Then he looked again to the darkening skies and said,

> "Look, Job—can anyone really understand the way the clouds are spread out above us?"[5]

The first sounds of distant thunder were heard, and again Elihu spoke.

> "Can anyone understand the thunder that rumbles within the clouds?"[6]

Great bolts of lightning flashed across the sky.

> "Look how God spreads the lightning around Him and even blankets the tops of the mountain with its flashes. . . . It looks like God fills His hands with lightning bolts like we might do with little darts, and then hurls them at His targets."[7]

> "Job, this thunder and this lightning are awesome—
>
> so loud
>   so near
>   so ominous
>   so frightening
> it's like—it's like—I feel the presence of God in this thunder."[8]

Elihu continued to give us one of the most graphic descriptions of an approaching storm to be found anywhere in all of literature—and without knowing it, he was describing the arrival of God. For God is approaching in all the "Pomp & Circumstance" of a grand processional, to the accompaniment of the rolling thunder and the flashing lightning.

Elihu said,[9]

> "My heart trembles."
> "Listen to the thunder of His voice."
> "It rolls across the heavens and His lightning flashes out in every direction."
> "This is glorious."
> "God is doing this, Job."
> "Look, Job, man is stopping his work."
> "The animals are hiding."
> "It may be that God is about to punish you, Job, or it may be that He is about to reward you."

Elihu then continued to describe the heavens, darkened with the tempest, dazzled by the lightning, and split apart by the thunder.

Suddenly, to the north, the sky brightened, as in a sunrise, as the illuminating presence of God in His resplendent glory approached.

Elihu said:[10]

> "As we cannot look at the sun for its brightness, neither can we gaze at the terrible majesty of God breaking forth upon us from heaven."
> "Look, Job, He's clothed in dazzling splendor."
> "His power is incomprehensible."
> "It's a wonder He does not destroy us."
> "No wonder men everywhere fear Him."

And Elihu finally ran out of words—poetic language failed him. His thoughts became disjointed, punctuated by his feelings as he described the approach of God—and then the sounds of wind and thunder took on coherence and meaning, and the deep rumblings from the clouds and high-pitched whine of a whirling tornado translated itself into meaningful words. As from the midst of an awesome storm, God began to speak.

**All of our arguments
cease when God
makes His appearance.**

Chapter Seven

A New and Unexpected Pain

I was returning from a speaking engagement a number of years ago. It was 2:00 in the morning—raining—and I was tired. The streets of Portland were deserted.

I drove through a red light. As soon as I realized what had happened, I skidded to a stop in the middle of the intersection. I looked each way and then inched through the remaining few feet of the intersection and proceeded to drive home.

The only other car within miles was a city police car.

The officer stopped me and gave me a ticket.

As I waited for the day of my court appearance to arrive, I became increasingly hostile—incensed—filled with reasons why I felt the fine was unjust.

For days I rehearsed my speech before the judge.

"I fell asleep," I would say.

"I was tired."

"There was no traffic."

"I did stop—it was a little late, but I did stop and then felt it safer to go forward than backward."

You know—all the regular excuses.

I arrived at the courthouse, convinced that I could "beat this rap."

The moment I entered that courtroom, I felt myself in the grip of

> something awesome—
>   something frightening
>   something terribly intimidating.

The focal point of the room was a high oak bench, behind which sat a stern-faced, black-robed figure of a man. His steely eyes seemed to penetrate the very depths of my soul.

He spoke with wisdom and with finality. When his gavel banged that desk-top, all argument ceased, judgment had been dispensed, the sentence was fixed, there seemed no recourse.

As I waited for my name to be called, I felt all the hostility seeping out of my pores. My arguments seemed so childishly inadequate. In the presence of the judge, I felt a strange combination of awesome respect and downright terror.

Finally my name was called. The charge was read, the judge lifted his eyes, peered right down into my naked soul, and asked, "How do you plead, guilty or not guilty?"

All of my rehearsed speeches vanished, and in their place I heard a small, timid, distant voice meekly answer, "Guilty, your Honor."

For months Job had been pleading for an audience with God. Time and again he appealed for a hearing.

> He had rehearsed his speech.[1]
> He had his questions memorized.[2]
> He was ready to make his accusations.[3]

And then God appeared.

Job was silent. There was not even the small, timid, distant voice. There was not even a squeak—Job was silent.

Until Job heard the voice of God emerging from the whirling of the wind—he had seen God as just another man—oh, bigger and greater and stronger and older and wiser, but just another man.

His God had been shrunken in size to fit the limited confines of his own finite mind—but now God appeared—and spoke—and Job was awed—and Job was silent.

Something always happens when God reveals Himself to man.

Something profound
    something different
        something life-changing
            something that's eternally unforgettable.

The terror, the dismay, the guilt that Job felt and later described seems to be a common response to God's appearance.

Adam hid.[4]
Abraham fell prostrate on the ground.[5]
Moses covered his face.[6]
Isaiah repented.[7]
Ezekiel fell.[8]
Daniel lapsed into a coma.[9]
Saul of Tarsus fell to the ground—
    his eyes were blinded
    his self-righteousness exposed
    his will was broken, and
    his spirit surrendered.[10]

All of our arguments cease when God makes His appearance.

All of Job's complaints were forgotten the moment God spoke.

If it had been possible to relive those months of complaining, I'm sure that Job never would have asked for an audience with God. The greatest pain Job felt was the pain of his own spiritual nakedness as he stood exposed to the all-seeing eye, the all-knowing mind, the ever-loving heart of the Almighty God.

For the first time in his life this good man—this just man—this blameless man—this upright man—this holy man of Uz—saw himself as God saw him.

God is not
only powerful,
but also just—
not only omnipotent,
but also right
in all that He does.

Chapter Eight

Questions That Answer Questions

I'm amazed at what God said. I am doubly amazed at what He did not say.

There was no rebuke, there was no pity, and there was no explanation.

He never did address Job's question, "Why?"

He never did honor Job's complaints.

Instead, God answered Job's question with some questions of His own[1]—seventy of them, to be exact. And He began with the one question that's designed to end all questions—He thunders the one sentence that puts man in his place—and God in His—

> "Who is this that darkens counsel by words without knowledge?"
>   or
> "Who is this that questions My providence?"
>   or
> "Who is this who claims to know more than I do?"

Job questioned God's wisdom, so now God questioned Job's wisdom. Then God threw out a challenge to Job—"You wanted a confrontation, you wanted a face-off—you've got it."

"Stand on your feet."
"Hitch up your belt."
"Roll up your sleeves."
"Let's fight."

Job, who questioned God, was now being forced to answer—or rather forced to admit he could not answer—questions that were basic and fundamental to God; questions to which God not only knew the answers, but questions formed by God before answers were available; questions uniquely designed to reveal to Job that he was but a man and that the One addressing him was truly God.

"Where were you when I laid the foundation of the Earth? Tell me if you know so much."

"Do you know how its dimensions were determined?"

"Do you know who did the surveying?"

"Do you know what supports its foundations and who laid its cornerstone during that time when the morning stars sang together and all the angels shouted for joy?"

"Do you know who decided the boundaries of the seas when they gushed up from the depths?"

"Do you know who clothed them with the clouds?"

"Have you ever commanded the sun to rise in the morning?"

"Have you ever robed the dawn in red?"

"Can you locate the gates of death?"

"Can you tell Me where the light comes from—or the darkness?"

"But of course you know all of this, don't you? For you were born before it was all created, weren't you?"

"Job, have you ever explored the treasures of the snow or the hail?"

"Where does the light come from? Where does the wind come from?"

"Who dug the valley for the torrents of rain?"

"Who laid the path for the lightning?"

"Who causes the rain to fall on the barren deserts, so that the parched and barren ground is satisfied with water?"

"Has the rain a father? Where does the dew come from?"

"Whose mother is the ice and frost?"

"Can you hold back the stars? Can you restrain the constellations of Orion and the Pleiades?"

"Can you control the seasons?"

"Do you know how mountain goats give birth?"

"Will the wild ox be your happy servant?"

"Do you know why an ostrich has no true motherly love?"

"Have you given the horse strength, or clothed his neck with quivering mane?"

"Do you know how a hawk soars . . . and is able to spread her wings to the south?"

"Do you still want to argue with me, Job? Or will you yield? Do you—God's critic—have the answer?"[2]

God has just taken a quick swing through all of creation—the earth, the heavens, and then a fleeting glimpse of His creative handiwork with some of His living creatures. He asked only the most basic questions. Job was still speechless.

Finally, the one who had attempted to bring God down to the size of man found himself shrinking and was forced to admit—

"I am nothing"

"I have no answers"

"I have said too much already."[3]

Restlessly, like a tiger pursuing its prey, God began again—

"Stand up and brace yourself for battle.
Let me ask you a question and you give Me the answer." [4]

God proceeded to ask moral questions of Job—questions that require a level of discernment found only in God Himself.[5]

"Are you going to discredit My justice and condemn Me, so that you can say that you are right?" Or, Job, do you wish to continue to maintain that I have allowed your pain without a reason in mind?

"Are you as strong as God, and can you shout as loudly as He?" Or, Job, do you think you can out-shout Me in maintaining that your suffering is unreasonable?

"Do you really have greater moral discernment than I?"

God then invited Job to put on the robes of royalty, ascend the throne, and make some routine judgments.[6]

> "How would you handle the proud? How does one determine who is truly proud? What sort of correction would you design in order to make them humble? Could you do it with a glance?"

> "How about the wicked? How would you determine who is truly wicked? What punishment would you uniquely design for each one?"

God then drew Job's attention to two animals—Behemoth,[7] a land animal, and Leviathan,[8] a sea animal.

Some commentators think that Behemoth is a hippopotamus and that Leviathan is a crocodile. Some think they are real, others think they are mythical. Some say they are symbolic. Whatever they are, it appears that Job knew about them and God described them as

> awesome,
>> frightening, and
>>> formidable.

Of Behemoth, God said, "No one can catch him off guard—no one can put a ring in his nose and lead him away."
Of Leviathan, God said,

> "It's useless to try to capture him."
> "No one dares stir him up."
> "When he stands up, the strongest are afraid. Terror grips them."
> "There is nothing so fearless anywhere on earth. Of all the beasts, he is the proudest—the monarch of all that he sees."

What God was saying with such clarity and such devastating forcefulness to Job is this:

> "No one can stand up to Me,"[9] and Job—
>> if you can't handle Behemoth—
>> if you can't handle Leviathan—
>> if you can't solve the moral problems of humanity—
>> if you can't even answer the most basic questions about creation—about life—
> How can you stand up to Me?
> How dare you challenge me?

Job is devastated.

Job is ashamed.

Job is finally ready to admit that he's no match for God—that even if God did answer his questions, he probably would be unable to understand.

He had only asked, "Why."

But even God's answers, as well as His questions, are beyond human comprehension.

Job said, "I know that You can do anything and that no one can stop you."[10]

God is not only powerful, but also just; not only omnipotent, but also right in all that He does; beyond dispute; beyond complaint. Job has finally eliminated the distortion and placed God in clear and sharp focus.

And then he finally answered one of God's questions—the only one God really wanted him to answer—the only one he was qualified to answer.[11] He said, "You ask who it is who has so foolishly denied Your providence. It is I. I was talking about things I knew nothing about and did not understand—things far too wonderful for me."

> "I do not even know enough to question God," said Job.
>
> "I'm too ignorant to even complain intelligently."
>
> "I thought I knew God—but it was only hearsay. All of my information was gleaned from others—but now," said Job, "I have seen You."
>
> "And I have seen myself, and I loathe myself and repent in dust and ashes."

I find it difficult to even comment on this scene. For God is taking a good man, a man worthy of His highest commendation, and making him better. God is taking one of His chosen ones and perfecting him. He's taking Job through that very private and very wonderful experience of purging and purifying. He is gently lifting him in and out of the fire, burning away the dross, and preparing to display him as one perfected through suffering.

Job is enduring the experience that most of us need and all of us fear: the painful but glorious experience of truly getting to know ourselves and truly getting to know our God.

**The only thing
God withheld
from Job
was an answer
to the perplexing
question, "Why?"**

Chapter Nine

The Unanswered Question

Job never did get his answer. He still didn't know why he had lost his herds, his flocks, his servants, his children, and his health.

But he did get them all back and more.

As God began to vindicate Job, He started with Job's accusers. He charged them with gross misrepresentation, declared His anger, and demanded a sacrifice for sin. He even denied them the privilege of offering their own sacrifice. The privilege was reserved for Job.

Job accepted their seven bulls and seven rams and then offered them to God, at the same time praying for their forgiveness. They were forgiven for the incorrect things they had said about God and the unjust things they had said concerning Job.[1]

At that precise moment, the moment of repentance and forgiveness, the miracles of restoration began.[2] Job's brothers, sisters, former friends, and even Job's wife returned. Job's health was restored. Job's wealth was replaced. Each of his visitors brought him a gift of money and a gold ring.

This godly man—

who had lost all of his 7,000 sheep . . . received 14,000 in return.

who had lost all of his 3,000 camels . . . received 6,000 in return.

who had lost all of his 500 oxen . . . received 1,000 in return.

who had lost all of his 500 female donkeys . . . received 1,000 in return.

Job's happiness was regained.

This proud father who had lost all of his ten children received ten more in return—again seven sons and three daughters—twenty in all—ten in heaven and ten on earth.

A double portion—freely given and joyfully received.

God even doubled his life span. We don't know for sure, but it is generally believed that Job was 70 years of age when tragedy struck. God graciously gave him 140 more, so that he was able to watch his children and his children's children to four generations.[3]

"Then at last he died, an old, old man, after living a long, good life."[4]

God had given Job all that he'd lost and all that he'd wanted. He vindicated him before all of his family and friends. He even gave him time out of His busy schedule for a private audience with Himself. He addressed him personally and face to face.

The only thing God withheld from Job—the only thing He refused to give him—was an answer to the perplexing question, "Why?"

Part 2

LEARNING FROM SUFFERING

———————————

There are times when
it's necessary for God
to appear to be
the "loser" on earth
in order to be
the "winner"
of unseen battles
taking place
in the heavens.

———————————

Chapter Ten

The View from the Top

But we know why, don't we? We had a look behind the scenes. We were given a view from the top. Early in his story we had a privileged "peek" over the shoulder of life's Script writer as He inserted a scene in the life of Job that explained it all.

I enjoy reading Paul Harvey's *The Rest of the Story*. Each time I read about those seldom-known facts in the lives of well-known people, I feel like I'm one of a privileged few who is being told intimate secrets known only to a select group.

God told us the rest of the story when He described the two times that He and Satan discussed the destiny of Job—the two times Satan questioned God's sovereignty and Job's integrity—the two times Satan claimed to be holding a trump card—the two times that God called his bluff and won.

It happened sometime in Eternity past. God was having one of His routine staff meetings in Heaven, discussing the conditions of His worlds, when Satan, the god of this world, appeared.[1]

Satan was taking a break from his routine supervision of earth[2] when God asked: "Have you noticed my servant, Job? He is the finest man in all the earth—a good man who fears God and will have nothing to do with evil."[3]

With characteristic cynicism Satan replied, "Why shouldn't he, when You pay him so well? You have always protected him and his home and his property from all harm. You have prospered everything he does—look how rich he is! No wonder he worships you. But just take away his wealth, and he will curse You to Your face."[4]

God called Satan's bluff. He said, "You may do anything you like with his wealth, but don't harm him physically."[5]

It was then that tragedy struck the first time. It was then that all of his herds and all of his flocks were lost—that most of his servants were slain—and all of his children died.

It was then that Job said,

> "Naked I came from my mother's womb, and
>   naked I shall return there.
> The Lord gave and the Lord has taken away.
> Blessed be the name of the Lord."[6]

It was then that it was said of Job, "Through all this Job did not sin nor did he blame God."[7]

Satan never learns, nor do his children. A second time he approached the throne of Heaven. God, with characteristic pride and delight in His children, said to Satan, "Well, have you noticed my servant Job? He is the finest man in all the earth—a good man who fears God and turns away from all evil. And he has kept his faith in Me despite the fact that you persuaded Me to harm him without a cause."[8]

Again Satan threw down a challenge. "Skin for skin," he replied, "a man will give anything to save his life. Touch his body with sickness, and he will curse You to Your face."[9]

Satan was convinced that Job's whole life was a lie: his faithful service for God, his unimpeachable character, his meaningful community involvement were all for selfish reasons. If only he could get through that "facade of holiness," he could then reveal the true Job as nothing but a fraud.

Again God called his bluff. "Do with him as you please," the Lord replied, "only spare his life."[10]

Now that Satan had permission to afflict his body, he began searching for the most effective method of human torture at his disposal:

> If he could just hurt him, endlessly—
>   if he could just isolate him, permanently—
>   if he could just brainwash him, incessantly—

ne was convinced that he could extract a confession that would expose Job and dishonor God.

I can imagine that his decision was explored with great care. This was a rare opportunity, and he must not fail. I'm sure he convened his trusted demons, and together they probably considered every possibility—the Chinese water-torture, the bamboo slips beneath the fingernails, and all of the other hideous and inhumane methods that man has invented to hurt man. Finally they chose one that they all felt was most appropriate—one designed

> to hurt
>> to separate
>>> to confuse
>>>> to humiliate
>>>>> to shame and . . .
>>>>> to linger,

one ultimately designed to destroy Job's spirit without destroying his body. It would be a torture that combined deep spiritual depression with an interminable excruciating physical pain—a torture that appeared to offer no possible hope of relief and that forced one to endure alone.

It was then that the itching began. It was then that his body became inflamed with a sore and angry swelling. It was then that red spots covered his flesh—

> his bones ached
>> his legs began to thicken
>>> his hair fell out
>>>> his face swelled, and
>>>>> his voice became hoarse.

It was then that his entire appearance changed until his face became grim and distorted, and his skin was encrusted and constantly running with pus.

It was then that his wife left him—his friends deserted him, and he was banished to the local garbage dump like refuse from under the kitchen sink, to begin his long journey into the living hell that refused to release him.

But Job didn't know that part of the story. There's no indication that Job ever heard of that heavenly confrontation.

He asked God repeatedly for a reason behind his pain, but God never answered that question. He never described the challenge thrown down by Satan.

He never explained the greater contest being run in full view of the spiritual world. He never discussed the "high stakes" that had been laid on Heaven's table as God "put his money on Job."

Job never knew—before, during, or after—the full reason for his suffering.

He was forced to suffer just as we are forced to sometimes suffer—without an explanation.

He knew, as we know, that suffering is a part of the human experience.

He knew, as we know, that suffering is tied to sin.

He knew, as we know, that suffering is part of God's corrective discipline—part of the purifying process.

He knew, as we know, that suffering in this world is unavoidable.

But when he had fully examined his life and his ways, and even after he had taken whatever corrective measures he felt necessary, the suffering persisted. It was then that he not only pled for his own sake, but also for the sake of God. He believed that God's honor was at stake. God was being forced to sit in the ashes, and that was no place for his God.

Little did he realize that there are times when it's necessary for God to appear to be the loser on earth in order to be the winner of unseen battles taking place in the heavens.

Job didn't know the story of a crucifixion that bore all the marks of defeat. All Job knew was that something unexplainable was happening. And there are times when that is all we are privileged to know.

**The battle was not
between Satan and Job,
but between
Satan and God.**

Chapter Eleven

Who Is Fighting This War?

Satan's goal was not to destroy Job, it was to discredit God.

This brief glimpse into the heavenly war was but a small part of the continuing conflict between Satan and God.

Job meant nothing to Satan. Job was merely an object—a target—a means to an end.

Job assumes the impersonal stature of a foot soldier in the front lines, a prisoner in a concentration camp. He is seen only as an impediment to the larger goal of gaining a strategic victory. In this instance Satan wanted to discredit God by causing one of His trusted servants to renounce Him completely.

That was the meaning of the words, "to curse God."[1]

To curse is not to swear or to use profane or even obscene language.

It does not mean to complain, or even criticize. It does not mean to question. It does not mean to get angry.

Screaming "ouch" when you stub your toe is not cursing God.

One of the tragic interpretations of Job has encouraged people to suffer in silence. It has heaped guilt upon them when they dared to ask God a question or to suggest to God that they would like some relief.

I resent the phrase, "don't cry," and its companion phrase, don't talk."

Tears are therapeutic and talk is therapeutic. God has given us tear ducts and tongues, and they become a very real part of the relief process when we hurt. And Job employed both.

So many feel some sort of sadistic heroism when they can suppress their true feelings as they're suffering, only to find that those bottled emotions eventually explode in all directions later on in life.

To curse God means to accuse God of unfaithfulness. It means to accuse God of not keeping His word—of being untruthful. But it means more. It means not only to accuse Him of unfaithfulness, but to turn away from Him in search of another god who might be more worthy of our confidence.

This was a typical heathen practice in Job's day—and in ours. Whenever a worshiper made expensive offerings to his god, he expected something from his god in return. He expected that god to prosper him and to protect him. If that god failed, he would then destroy that god or reject that god—or curse that god.

Cursing god meant to exchange one god for another as we might fire our stockbroker if he fails to make a wise investment, or our realtor if he's unable to sell our house.

Satan has never been noted for his high and lofty thoughts about God. He has always felt that he is God's superior or at least His equal. He's always been convinced that he knows the mind of God and even what the limitations of God are.

One great mistake that Satan has always made has been in his assumption that God is limited like himself. Another has been in assuming that God's servants are just like his own: opportunists that can be bought, hypocrites that live their lives only on the surface, proud people that can never condone being humbled.

Satan measured God and His children by his own standards and found himself horribly mistaken.

The more he crushed Job, the more Job emitted a fragrance that both startled Satan and pleased God; the more he stretched Job and squeezed Job, the louder Job cried his allegiance to his God—until, when it was all finished, Satan fled from God's presence like a whipped puppy. Cowering in the corner of the universe, Satan was forced to watch a vindicated man and a glorified God as they continued to walk together in a totally satisfying relationship.

In case you're worried that when your turn comes, you won't be able to "hang on" like Job, let me remind you—the battle was not between Satan and Job; it was between Satan and God.

Job gets a lot of credit, but that's because God chose to give it to him. It's interesting that this is always God's way.

God does the work—but man gets the credit.

That's just like our God, isn't it?

Jesus said, "Without me, you can do nothing."[2] And then He promised the faithful sufferer that "your reward is great in heaven. . . ."[3] If God is the enabler and Christ is the strengthener, it would seem Theirs should be the reward. But no, God does the work, and He gives us the credit.

I can remember when I was teaching my son John to play golf. He could barely hold the club. I would reach my arms around him, take his hands in mine—grip the club, address the ball, and then swing. Whenever we would hit that ball, and it would sail through the air for any significant distance, I would always clap and cheer and pat him on the back, and say, "John, look what *you* did. Great work, Son!"

Now we both knew the truth, and you know the truth. God knows the truth about any spiritual achievements we accomplish in this life. God does the work, but He still chooses to give us the credit.

Job did not curse God, because of the unfailing grace of God in his life; because of the undeserting presence of God in his life; because of the unyielding power of God in his life.

The tribute belongs to God—not to Job; because the war was God's, not Job's, just as it is in our lives.

The outcome was God's, too. And whenever the ultimate purpose and goal is determined by God, the outcome is always predictable.

Satan is a loser—God is a winner. And God has already predicted the outcome for us all. Why? Because we're strong? Because we're faithful? No! Because He is strong and He is faithful and He is able to "keep that which is committed to Him."[4]

Martha and I were talking about God's grace one day when she said, "I don't think that I have dying grace, and it worries me." I said, "We don't need dying grace when we're living. When it comes time to die, the grace will be there."

Many of us worry that we don't have suffering grace. We don't need suffering grace when we're rejoicing. But when it becomes time to suffer, the grace will be there—just as it was when it was Job's time to suffer.

Don't fret. God will hold you up, too, just as He did Job.

**No suffering
can touch the believer
without having first
received
the permission of God.**

Chapter Twelve

How to Prepare for Suffering

If you're planning to suffer any time in the near future—and none of us is, though most of us will—then you'd better be sure that your theology is correct.

Our response to suffering is determined by our understanding of God.

What we think about God will influence how we respond to trials in this lifetime.

If you feel like many, that Job's great loss in life was something that Satan slipped by God while He was busy elsewhere, or that Job's suffering was something unavoidable—something God could not help—then you could easily give up in despair.

But if you see God as the God of the Bible—

> supreme
> sovereign, and
> sensitive,

not allowing trials except by Divine permission, then you can see purpose, even if you do not know what that purpose is. The Christian life is kept fine-tuned by biblical theology.

We should always interpret experience by truth—we should always filter every pain through the lens of deity. When God is in sharp focus, then life is also undistorted.

Harold S. Kushner wrote a book, *When Bad Things Happen to Good People*, published by Avon books in 1981, that very quickly became an acclaimed national bestseller. Rabbi Kushner explores the question, "Why?" as he relives the painful experience of his son Aaron's suffering and death. The book is well-written, extremely interesting, and easy to read. The only problem is its theology.

It presents God as a reactive force in the universe, not always in complete control. It describes a god, unlike the God of the Bible, who really doesn't always know what's happening.

He asks the question, "Could it be that God does not cause the bad things to happen to us?"[1]

He then explores the Book of Job for the answer to his own question. In what he considers to be the "Job-fable,"[2] he concludes that "bad things do happen to good people in this world, but it is not God who wills it. God would like people to get what they deserve in life, but He cannot always arrange it."[3]

He suggests that "God wants the righteous to live peaceful, happy lives, but sometimes even He can't bring that about. It is too difficult even for God to keep cruelty and chaos from claiming their innocent victims."[4]

He concludes by encouraging us to "forgive God despite His limitation, as Job does, and as we once learned to forgive and love our parents even though they were not as wise, as strong, and as perfect as we needed them to be."[5]

I recently saw an ad for the movie "The Incredible Shrinking Woman." It's the story of a woman who, for some reason, begins to shrink.

In fact, the woman shrinks until she becomes so small that climbing up onto her bed becomes an impossible task.

Chair legs and table legs appear like skyscrapers to her.

Her great fear is that she will be captured and eaten by her pet kitten.

She finally falls into the kitchen sink and is sucked into the garbage disposal.

Harold Kushner, like many today who cannot comprehend the incomprehensible, tends to shrink God down and down and down to man's size and then attempts to describe Him in terms of man's understanding.

The result is that the Bible's God is eventually and completely lost to the very people to whom it was addressed.

Job had a low view of God.

Job thought God treated His servants as men do—that simply because he couldn't understand the reason for his suffering, God was having one of His capricious, unpredictable mood-swings and punishing him without a reason.[6]

Job needed to fully understand the uniqueness of God.

Elihu reminded Job of his foolishness by saying, "God is greater than man . . . He does not give an account of His doings."[7] But Job did not understand that.

Job also thought that because God was silent, it meant that He was absent.[8] Job needed David's perspective on the abiding presence of God. David said,

> "Where can I go from Thy Spirit? Or where can I flee from Thy presence?
>
> If I ascend to heaven, Thou art there;
> If I make my bed in Sheol, behold, Thou art there.
>
> If I take the wings of the dawn,
> If I dwell in the remotest part of the sea,
>
> Even there Thy hand will lead me."[9]

Job could have added one more verse to David's beautiful Psalm. He could have said,

> "Even if I am forced from my home to lie in the dust and ashes of the local garbage dump of Uz—Thou art there."

God *was* there—hearing—watching—waiting for the right moment to move in on the wings of the wind and restore Job.

I'll never forget how God transformed a miserable little cubicle in the psychiatric ward of a Veteran's Hospital into a sanctuary by simply giving to me a sense of His presence.

Spending Easter Sunday in a foxhole in New Guinea became a rich and rewarding experience simply by enjoying a sense of divine presence.

Brother Lawrence teaches us that the most miserable or the most mundane experiences of life can be transformed by "Practicing the Presence of God."

Job thought that since there was no understandable reason for his sufferings, there must be no purpose.[10]

Job failed to comprehend the sovereignty of God—at first. When God finally revealed Himself, Job's declaration became

one of the grandest definitions for sovereignty to be found anywhere. He stated,

> "I know that You can do anything and that no one can
> stop you."[11]

Job acknowledged active divine involvement in his pain—
without knowing why. He finally conceded that God, for some
unknown reason, was in charge and in control.

The Book of Job presents a view of very active divine involvement in human suffering. That involvement, as we review
the challenge thrown down by Satan, was in the form of divine
approval.

Before Satan could lift a finger to touch Job, or his possessions, it was first necessary to gain God's permission.

This means that God allowed Job to suffer. He did not will
it to happen, any more than He did not forbid it to happen, any
more than He forbade Adam and Eve to eat the forbidden
fruit—He allowed it to happen.

God allows us to suffer. This may be the only solution to
the problem that we will ever receive.

Nothing can touch the Christian without having first received the permission of God. If I do not accept that statement,
then I really do not believe that God is sovereign—and if I do
not believe in His sovereignty, then I am helpless before all the
forces of heaven and hell. I am subject to the capricious whims
of anyone or anything that might desire to harm me.

When Jesus was about to be crucified, Pilate said to Him,
"Do you not know that I have the authority to release you, and I
have the authority to crucify you?"

Jesus answered, "You have no authority over Me, unless it
has been given to you from above. . . ."[12]

Pilate could not lift a finger against the life of Jesus Christ
without first having gained permission from God.

When Jesus was predicting Peter's denial, He said,
"Simon, Simon, behold, Satan has demanded permission to sift
you like wheat."[13]

Satan could not lift a finger against Peter without first having gained permission from God.

One summer Martha and I planned what we thought was
the perfect vacation. We secured the lovely vacation home of a
dear friend in central Oregon and planned to spend three uninterrupted weeks of resting, studying, bicycling, and enter-

taining our children. We both laid out our books, carefully placed the deck chairs, turned down the bed, flipped on the television, and began to enjoy some much needed rest.

The first evening we climbed on two bicycles and proceeded to explore Black Butte Ranch. Before the evening's ride was finished, I had broken three ribs, suffered a mild concussion and numerous abrasions on my arms and legs—I was a mess. I spent five days in a hospital.

Just before my release from the hospital, I developed a severe case of shingles.

There were times during the next few months that I was convinced that Job's boils were really the shingles in disguise.

Needless to say—our vacation plans were somewhat altered. There was no vacation as far as I was concerned. What had promised to be weeks of rest turned into months of torment.

Why? I haven't the slightest idea.

The only thing that I know for sure is that for some reason, unknown to me, God allowed both the accident and the shingles. That knowledge wasn't quite enough then; it took other things like doctors and medication and an attentive wife, but it's enough now.

God allows us to suffer, for nothing can touch the life of a Christian without first having received permission from the Father.

That knowledge of God may not lessen the pain, but it will ease considerably the anxiety that sometimes intensifies pain to the point where it is unbearable.

Let me repeat, if you're planning any experience of suffering in the near future, you'd better be sure that your theology is correct.

**No one can fully explain
God's actions
but God.**

Chapter Thirteen

Why?

What was wrong with the theology of Job's friends?

Eliphaz, Bildad, and Zophar made God angry. He said, "My wrath is kindled against you . . . because you have not spoken of Me what is right as my servant Job has."[1]

These three who had traveled so far, whose intentions were so honorable, whose desires were to comfort and to heal, were almost slain by God. They were accused of outright sin. They had not spoken correctly about God.[2]

First—they claimed to know the mind of God. Has anyone ever said to you, "I know why God allowed that to happen to you . . ." I've heard it many times.

When our son, Jimmy, died, one woman said, "God took your little boy because you did not have the faith to believe he would be healed. . . ."

When I broke out with the shingles, one man said, "This is God telling you to slow down."

While preaching in the Philippines, I became ill. A friend said, "God is trying to tell you to stop taking trips to foreign countries."

The only time I felt that one of these "interpreters of the divine" might be right was when I had my bicycle accident. My brother said, "I think God is telling you to stop riding bicycles." I agreed with him and have not climbed on one since.

No one knows the mind of God but God.

No one can fully explain God's actions but God.

The only certain understanding any of us has is what God has recorded of His thinking for us in the Scripture.

God has unique and wonderful ways of revealing His will to the body of believers and even to individual believers. But comprehending the divine reasons behind every divine action is reserved for God Himself.

Eliphaz, Bildad, and Zophar had it all figured out. They agreed—they sustained their argument—they never backed down, they said it over and over again—"God is punishing you because you have sinned!"

Everything that follows that opening remark is repetitious—just the same words over again—like a broken record—amplified and intensified—but nothing new and nothing different.

It is sheer human arrogance to claim this kind of knowledge.

It is the ultimate in human pride.

It is effrontery to God and causes embarrassment to the body of Christ.

Only God knows the mind of God.

When people continue to ask me Why? Why? Why?—

Why did God allow my child to die?
Why did God allow me to lose my job?
Why did God permit my business to go bankrupt?

The most God-honoring thing I can answer is . . . "I do not know." There may be human explanations, but as for God's reasons behind God's actions, they are a mystery to me, for . . .

"His understanding is infinite."[3]
and
"There is no searching of His understanding . . ."[4]
and says the Apostle Paul,
"Oh, the depth of the riches both of the wisdom and knowledge of God! How unsearchable are His judgments and unfathomable His ways."[5]

Eliphaz, Bildad, and Zophar did not and could not know, for sure, what God was doing in Job's life and why.

Second—they handcuffed God and stuffed Him into their own little man-made theological box.

They had one simple thesis—and no more. Their theology stated that

> "Prosperity is God's reward for righteousness,"
>   and
> "Suffering is God's judgment for sin."
> "If you live right you will be blessed.
>   If you sin you will be cursed."

The word sovereign suggests freedom. It teaches that God is free to do as He pleases and when He pleases. The only limitations of that freedom come from those restrictions that God's very nature has placed upon Himself.

To suggest that God must act and react in exactly the same way to everyone, everywhere, is to rob God of His sovereignty.

As I study the Scriptures and recall my own life experiences, I'm convinced that God delights in keeping us off balance by never employing the same attention-getting device more than once in a lifetime.

Eliphaz, Bildad, and Zophar portrayed God as inflexible, with His ways set in concrete. In their view, He was unable to break from His rigidity long enough to suit a unique, one-of-a-kind experience and capture the attention of a unique, one-of-a-kind person. God said,

> "For as the heavens are higher than the earth, so are
>   My ways higher than your ways and My thoughts
>   than your thoughts."[6]

Third—these three men worshiped a God who was a theological cripple, a God who limped along with the leg of His severity much, much longer than the leg of His goodness.

They saw God as some sort of a cosmic judge, ready to "zap" anyone and everyone who took one wrong step.

They saw Him as mean and unforgiving, with

> no compassion,
>   no mercy,
>   no grace,
>   no goodness,
>   no patience, and
>   no love.

They saw

> only the severity of God,
>> only the righteousness of God,
>>> only the holiness of God,
>>>> only the Law of God,

and completely ignored

> His love,
>> His mercy,
>>> His goodness, and
>>>> His grace.

They were theologically off-balance—as we are most of the time.

Many of us who have grown up in evangelical homes have been overbalanced in the same direction. We call it legalism. We have found it difficult to move from a fear of God to a love for God—to enjoy God rather than be afraid of Him. We have been more obsessed with negatives than positives—with "should nots" rather than "shoulds."

I'm still breaking free of that theological stranglehold and finding freedom in Christ to be a most delightful experience.

The Bible describes God as a God of balance:

> Romans 11:22 balances goodness and severity.
> Psalm 85:10 describes the balance by saying,
>> "Lovingkindness and truth have met together;
>> Righteousness and peace have kissed each other."

Theological balance is always difficult.

But theological balance is always necessary if we are going to be able to stand up straight in a crippled world and adequately display our God to a limping civilization.

Eliphaz, Bildad, and Zophar were rebuked because they began talking about God long before they really had gotten to know Him.

—————————————

**If you're thinking about
death as the solution
to suffering,
be sure that first
you fully understand
what death is all about.**

—————————————

Chapter Fourteen

One Solution That Is No Solution

I have thought seriously of committing suicide. In the book, *Depression,*[1] written by Dr. Emery Nester and myself, I devoted an entire chapter to the subject.

It is always deeply embarrassing for me to recall those low times when I was held in the grip of an unrelenting depression—and found myself considering suicide as a means of escape.

Job wanted to die, too. I've found that at some time in our lives, most of us entertain the same wish.

Job says repeatedly that death is to be preferred to life.[2]

> "Why didn't I die at birth?"
> "Why did the midwife let me live?"
> "Oh, to have been stillborn! To have never breathed or seen the light."
> "Oh, why should light and life be given to those in misery and bitterness, who long for death, and it won't come; who search for death as others search for food or money!"

Job not only had a low view of God, he had a low view of death. Job viewed death as the world views death today. He saw it at times as the end—as a cessation of being—the termination of all—the conclusion of human existence.

He said,

> "For if only I had died at birth, then I would be quiet now, asleep and at rest . . ."
>
> "For there in death the wicked cease from troubling, and there the weary are at rest."
>
> "There even prisoners are at ease, with no brutal jailer to curse them."
>
> "Both rich and poor alike are there, and the slave is free at last from his master."
>
> "What blessed relief when at last they die!"[3]

Later he said,

> "I'm sick and near death, the grave is about to receive me."
>
> "My hope will go down with me to the grave. We shall rest together in the dust."[4]

He seemed to be unsure, however, of just what death held for him—just like our world today. In one place he said,

> "As water evaporates from a lake, as a river disappears in drought, so a man lies down for the last time, and does not rise again until the heavens are no more; he shall not awaken, nor be roused from his sleep."[5]

In another he said,

> "If a man dies, surely he won't live again! This thought gives me hope, so that in all my anguish I eagerly await sweet death!"[6]

And yet again his ambivalence—his uncertainty about death—was evident. He said,

> "And I know that after this body has decayed, this body shall see God! Then He will be on my side! Yes, I shall see Him, not as a stranger, but as a friend. What a glorious hope."[7]

He would swing from one conviction to another—confused—not really sure what death would mean to him.

If you're thinking of death, be sure that you know what it's all about before you make any plans to go there.

The church of Jesus Christ is a thoroughly competent travel agency, with plenty of road maps available. There is no need for uncertainty as to what to expect, or just how to get where you want to go.

Two of the speakers responded to Job's lingering wish to die.

Elihu pleaded with great emotion to Job:

> "Do not long for the night, when people vanish in their place."[8]

Please, Job, do not wish to die, he said.

God asked a question of Job:

> "Have the gates of death been revealed to you?
> Or have you seen the gates of deep darkness?"[9]

We have such a sterile, unrealistic view of death today.

We view make-believe death on the screen, and it looks so harmless.

We see death in the funeral home, and it looks so life-like. I like to take members of my staff to funerals with me—not only to watch the service, the interaction with family members, and to listen to the words of comfort—but also with the hope that I might take them from the viewing room to the embalming room and show them the unbelievable and marked contrast between real death and make-believe death.

The lifeless form of a dead person is a hideous, empty, unforgettable sight. Many have never seen real death—death without rouge and lipstick and mascara and skin coloring. It's awesome and frightening.

God asked Job:

> "Have the gates of death been revealed to you?
> Or have you seen the gates of deep darkness?"

Do you really know what death is like, Job? As hideous as physical death is, spiritual death is even worse. To be separated from the body is frightening, but to be separated from God is unthinkable.

In sharp contrast to what Job seems to think, the writer of Hebrews tells that death is not the place of rest—not the place of escape—not the place of release, but the place of judgment.

> ". . . it is appointed for men to die once, and after this comes judgment."[10]

Rest, release, and peace are reserved for those who have made arrangements to spend eternity with Christ in Heaven and are willing to wait and willing to allow God to play out His drama in their lives until that precise moment when He chooses to bring down the curtain and call them home.

If you're thinking about death as a solution to suffering, make sure that you fully understand all that God—Who holds the keys of life and death—has to say about it.

To complain is to
doubt God.
It is the same thing as
suggesting that God
really doesn't know
what He's doing.

Chapter Fifteen

Job's Sin

Did you ever accuse God of not knowing what He was doing?

Probably not in so many words—but to complain means the same thing. It's far from cursing God, but it is an accusation against God. It questions God's wisdom and God's good judgment.

It's called presumption. A complaint about any uncontrollable circumstance in life presumes that God is either absent or that He is not nearly as smart as we are.

To complain does not mean to discuss—or to explore—or to search for meaning. It does not mean to describe one's feelings or to appeal to others for insight or prayer or compassion.

To complain means that after investigation has been made of any uncontrollable circumstance, a charge is lodged against God. An accusation is hurled heavenward that suggests that God is unfair or unwise or unloving or even unconcerned about our needs.

Job complained—loudly, bitterly, incessantly. In fact, the word "complain" appears more times in the book of Job than in any other book of the Bible. Nearly one-half of the "complaints" in Scripture fall from the lips of Job.

He said:

> "I will complain in the bitterness of my soul."[1]
> ". . . I will give full vent to my complaint."[2]

With one bold stroke of his verbal pen, God brings the sin of Job's complaining into sharp relief when He says:[3]

> "Who is this that darkens counsel without knowledge?"
> or
> "Why are you using your ignorance to deny My providence?"
> or
> "Who is this that doubts My good judgment?"
> or
> "Who is this that claims to know more than I do?"
> or
> "Who is this that thinks he knows what's better for his life than I do?"
> or
> "Who is this that dares to question Me?"
> or
> "Who is this that accuses Me of not knowing what I am doing?"

With that one blazing question, God placed His divine finger on the single sin that marred and disfigured Job's whole experience of suffering—the one sin for which Job ultimately was forced to repent.

The enormity of the sin of complaining is described in Psalm 78 as God recounts for us the early experiences of Israel as they traveled from Egypt to Canaan.

> They complained when their leader was present.
> They complained when their leader was absent.
> They complained because they had no water.
> They complained because they had no food.
> When God provided food,
> They complained because they had no meat.
> They complained because their journey required time and
> effort and
> battles.
> They complained because God punished them for their complaining.

Israel's constant complaints angered God, and His wrath was kindled against them—why? Because God has always equated complaining with unbelief. He called it[4] "sin," "rebellion," "unbelief," "deception," and "treachery."

God reacted to their unbelief. He rebuked them, judged them, killed some of them, destroyed their crops, killed their cattle—He loved them, forgave them, was compassionate toward them, and restrained His anger time and again. Why?—because to complain is to doubt God. It's the same as to suggest that God really does not know what He is doing.

Israel loved the prospect of freedom. They loved the promise of a land "that flowed with milk and honey"[5]; they loved the thought of a place of their own, where they could worship Jehovah God—*but* Israel hated the process they were forced to endure in order to get there.

Job was delighted with the prospect of someday dying quietly in his own little nest after a long, good life—but Job hated his experience of suffering.

He loved the promise, but hated the process.

We revel in thoughts of Heaven, but the thought of dying is frightening, and we fight it until we can fight it no longer.

We love the promise, but hate the process.

We rejoice in the hope of perfection, but we struggle with the pain of perfecting.

We love the promise, but hate the process.

If only we could go from the promise to its fulfillment, without the process.

It's during the process of getting to where God has promised that we experience life's bitter complaints. We plod through circumstances that *seem* to have no bearing whatever on the "promise." It's then that we wonder if God has left us or if God really knows what He's doing.

Years ago I was invited to pastor a church in an area where I had never wanted to live. I was restrained from saying no.

One morning as I was reading from the book of Isaiah, a passage reached out, grabbed me, and refused to let me go.

It said some very relevant things to me. It suggested that

1. you will enjoy the land
2. your ministry will flourish and
3. your health will improve.

As I sat there rereading the passage, I wanted to resist the personal implications on good hermeneutical grounds. I knew that the promise was originally made to Israel, and I knew the dangers of tampering with a context—nevertheless, as I read I suddenly became aware that tears were flowing from my eyes.

Martha came in and sat beside me and asked, "Are we going?"

"Yes," I answered, "We're going." When I showed the passage to her, it seemed so appropriate, so right, and so exciting.

Months later I sat alone in my car on the outskirts of that city. It was desert, and I'd always hated desert. I loved green—green grass, green trees, green hills, and green mountains. But in that place everything was brown—brown soil, brown grass, brown houses, brown buildings, and no hills and no mountains.

I used to ride an elevator to the thirteenth floor of the tallest building in town just to see something—it was so flat.

And the ministry was hard. It was only nominally successful.

My health—I experienced more health problems there than anywhere. I spent four years in deep depression, ten weeks in a psychiatric ward. I was forced to resign because of continuing poor health.

All the time I was wondering—

> Where was God?
> Does God really know what He's doing?
>   or
> Did we misinterpret the signals?
>   or
> Did we misread the Scriptures?

From our present vantage point, Martha and I rejoice in a promise that we still feel was personally meant for us. The problem was that we didn't understand the process.

Today, many years later, we love the place of our ministry, my health has improved, and the work is flourishing. None of this would have been possible, however, without the process of a desert experience that included all the things we needed but had never expected and certainly never wanted.

I complained while in the desert.

I repented when I became aware of the enormity of my sin.

To complain about any circumstance in life—

> my health
>> my wealth (or lack of it)
>>> my success
>>>> my failure
>>>>> my job
>>>>>> my age
>>>>>>> my place of residence
>>>>>>>> my appearance
>>>>>>>>> my parents (or absence of them)
>>>>>>>>>> my singleness
>>>>>>>>>>> my married state
>>>>>>>>>>>> my children (or lack of them)
>>>>>>>>>>>> even the weather—

is an accusation against God's wisdom and God's good judgment; it presumes that God is either absent or that He is not nearly so smart as we are.

After listening silently to God and finally seeing himself "as nothing"[6] when compared with God, Job forgot his discomfort, fell back down amidst the garbage, and said, "I know that Thou canst do all things, and that no purpose of Thine can be thwarted."[7]

Job admitted that God was smarter, more competent, and far more discerning than he, and in so doing, Job acknowledged that God was far more capable of successfully running his life—even if the process included the experience of painful suffering.

When God appears, man changes.

Chapter Sixteen

Job's Victory

When God appears, man changes.

God's speech to Job, one of the longest Person-to-person visits recorded in Scripture, brought about a dramatic transformation.

> Job forgot his pain.
> > He ceased his wailing.
> > > He dropped his broken shards of pottery.
> > > > He stopped the scraping of his pus-encrusted body.
> > > > > He stopped shouting questions at God
> > > > > and accusations at his counselors.
> > > > > > He forgot the ashes
> > > > > > and the dung
> > > > > > and the garbage
> > > > > > and the lepers
> > > > > > and the dogs—

he was aware of only one thing—God was present—and when God appears man changes.

Man forgets the unimportant and the temporal—man remembers the significant and the eternal. Job saw himself.

For the first time in Job's life he saw himself. He said, "I am nothing."[1]

For a man of Job's stature to admit that he is nothing—was something.

On the surface one might question Job's self-concept and even argue with him. But it would be futile—for when one sees God and compares himself with God, the only conclusion is the one Job came to—"I am nothing."

Job saw God. For the first time in his life he saw God. His prior knowledge was all second-hand—somebody else's information or revelation, but not his own. It was hearsay—it was like most of the things we know about God; but now his information was his own—his understanding of God was unblurred, undistorted, and clearly focused.

He said, "I know You can do anything and that no one can stop You."[2] For the first time in his life,

> he saw God as completely sovereign
> he saw God as the gracious controller of all things
> he saw God as free—free to do
> > whatever He pleased
> > whenever He pleased—and without explanation.
> He saw God
> > behind all the events on earth and
> > above all supernatural powers in Heaven.
> He saw
> > the sovereign will and
> > > the sovereign power and
> > > > the sovereign purpose
> > > > > of the sovereign God, and

Job was no longer interested in answers; he was only interested in a relationship.

Whenever I leave home for any length of time, I always phone or write. My calls or letters are filled with questions and requests for information.

> How's the weather?
> How are the kids?
> Is the dog all right?
> How do you feel?
> Is everything OK at the church?

Just routine—even somewhat mundane.

But when I come home and walk through that door and take Martha in my arms, I don't waste time asking about the weather, or the kids, or the dog, or even the church.

I'm not interested in answers, I'm interested only in a relationship—and a relationship was what Job was enjoying.

He assumed the proper position—down, down again to the garbage and ashes.

The custom of dirt and ashes is somewhat like our custom of wearing black when we're in mourning. The ancients tried to appear on the outside the same way they felt on the inside.

So Job sat in the ashes again and then lifted handful after handful over his head and let it fall like rain down over his body until his flesh was the color of his soul—gray—the color of the ground beneath him.

God's ultimate intention for Job was not only repentance—it was also restoration. The restoration of Job's wealth and of Job's health was really no problem. That could have been accomplished as quickly as was his loss—in just one day.

To restore family and friends to a vindicated and healed Job posed no real problem.

> As soon as Job's health returned—
> as soon as his blemishes faded—
> as soon as the fear of infection was gone—
> as soon as he had shaved and showered

they would all come back.

Job's place in his community could be restored. He could fight his way back to the top. He could start over, and with the natural abilities God had heaped upon him, he could be successful again. But for one thing!

> Job had been offended
>   he had been deserted
>   he had been ridiculed
>   he had been humiliated
>   he had been wounded deeply—
>   permanently.

Could he forgive—

> His friends?
> His family?
> His wife?

The healing process could have been stopped right there.

The bitterness that was smoldering in the mind of Job could have continued and could have ignited into a full-scale fire that would have consumed him.

Can a man forgive a wife who deserts him in the time of his greatest need?

Can a man forgive relatives who will just stand back and allow tragedy to run its full course?

Can a man forgive would-be counselors who offer only criticism without compassion?

Can a man forgive such words as: "hypocrite," "arrogant," "wicked," "rebel," "blasphemer"?

In a previous pastorate of mine, a young man returned home from Vietnam minus one leg and one wife.

His leg had been blown off by a land mine, and his wife had deserted him when she heard of the severity of his wounds.

He hobbled into my office one day, threw his crutches against the wall, and said, "Pastor, I'm mad! I've never been so mad. I'm mad clear down to my bones! Everything I've ever wanted is gone—my wife, my career, my home, my future, even my self-respect. And I want to fight the whole world, or die—and I'm not sure which.

"I'm so tired of people looking on me with pity—thinking I'm helpless. Do you want to know how helpless I am? Come on, I'll show you."

He never gave me time to answer. He just picked up his crutches and began swinging that leg—and that stump—down the hall, out the door, and to the parking lot.

"Get in," he said. I climbed in, buckled my seat belt (firmly), and watched as he struggled in behind his automatic controls; and then he took off—50, 60, 70, 80, 90, 100 miles per hour. Down the back streets, through stop signs, blind intersections, unpaved alleys, completely ignoring danger.

He drove like a madman. Once he looked over at me and said, "Scared, preacher?" I wasn't scared—I was terrified. But I'd never admit it. "Am I supposed to be?" I asked.

Finally he stopped, laid his head on the steering wheel, and began to cry. Between the sobs he would look over at me and with hate-filled eyes said, "Don't talk to me about God—about love—about honor—about faith! Don't talk to me about forgiveness! Don't ask me to forgive my wife. I'll never forgive her for what she did to me!"

And, as far as I know, he never did.

As far as I know, he's still living with the fire of hate burning in his soul.

Job had that option.

Job could have reacted with great glee when God said to Eliphaz, "I am angry with you and with your two friends . . ."[3]

He could have said, "Go for it, God!—Tell him off! Give him what he deserves. Zap him." But he didn't.

Job could have refused when God instructed him to help offer sacrifices for their sins.[4]

Eliphaz, Bildad, and Zophar went to Job, they offered their sacrifices and Job offered his prayer—and the Lord accepted Job's prayer.[5]

What do you suppose Job prayed? The same thing Jesus prayed in His great suffering—"Father forgive them. . . ." That was the only prayer that God could have accepted. That was the prayer that cooled His anger—and Job could not have asked God to forgive them unless he had forgiven them himself.

It's impossible to ask God to forgive someone we will not forgive.

We never pray, "Father, please forgive so and so for what he's done to me—but don't expect me to. . . ."

No one asks God to be nice to someone when we plan not to be.

> Job prayed for them—
>   that means
> Job forgave them.

There is great freedom in forgiveness.

There is great release in being forgiven.

But, there is even a greater freedom—

That is the freedom of forgiving. That seems to be so hard for so many of us.

We can forgive most people once, twice, maybe three times, if the sin isn't too great. But after that—forgiveness becomes terribly difficult.

Our response to requests for forgiveness are so unlike God's—

> "I'll forgive you, but—"
> "I'll forgive you—just give me a little time."

"I'll forgive you this time, but don't let it ever happen
again!"

"I'll forgive you—I'm not sure I'll ever forget this, but
I'll forgive you."

Job had just seen God—

Job had just been forgiven the sin of questioning God's
providence—

Job's heart was full.

Job's anger was emptied, and

Job forgave—

> his wife
> > his friends
> > > his relatives
> > > > his counselors—

Job forgave them all.

And then—Job was restored. Not a moment before. "Then
when Job prayed for his friends, the Lord restored his wealth
and his happiness! In fact, the Lord gave him twice as much as
before!"[6]

**If there is anything
a sufferer needs,
it is not an explanation,
but a fresh, new look
at God.**

Chapter Seventeen

Job's Satisfaction

Does God really owe us an explanation for what He does? Job thought so.

Martha and I thought so when Jimmy died. The only word that seemed to fall from our lips during those bewildering days was the word, "Why?" We asked it of God, of ourselves, of each other, and we asked it of anyone who took the time to listen to us speak from our grief.

Like Mary and Martha we instinctively questioned God—not for long—but we did question God. Do you remember Martha's first words to Jesus after her brother Lazarus had died? John 11:21 records them. "Lord, if You had been here, my brother would not have died."[1] Mary said the same thing a few moments later. "Lord, if You had been here, my brother would not have died."[2]

Those stinging words of accusation, directed at the very heart of God, really didn't catch Jesus by surprise. Human reactions to any circumstance have always been predictable to God.

And yet, when those two sisters—close friends of Jesus—charged Him with gross negligence, unnecessary delay, and unexplained absence to the point of actually contributing to the death of their brother, it must have taken some toll on the sensitive, loving nature of the Son of God.

We all question God when tragedy strikes.

> It's inbred—
>> it's innate—
>>> it's normal—
>>>> it's natural.

A question, in its spontaneous, unrehearsed form comprises a temporary tribute to God.

> It says that we believe there is a God.
> It says that we believe He knows.
> It says that we believe He cares.
> It says that we believe He controls.
> It says many things that we often forget to say to Him
> or about Him in the normal course of everyday life.

In the temporary insanity that deep grief causes, we lash out at everyone and everything in a vain attempt to find answers and, if possible, to change circumstances.

Did you notice in John 11 how Jesus responded to their words?

He made no reference to them: No rebuke, no shame, no charge—just silence—and then He proceeded to teach them something far more important about life and death.[3]

We even blame ourselves.

When Jimmy died, we often pointed the finger of blame at ourselves. "If only we had prayed harder," or "if only we had taken him to a doctor sooner," or "if," "if," "if," and yet we were told that his death was unavoidable.

I became irritated with Jimmy's constant crying the night before his death. I spoke sharply to him. Imagine, a grown man rebuking a three-month old son for crying when he hurt—nevertheless, I did it. I often look back upon that moment with regret and guilt and shame and wish I could recall those words. I even wonder if maybe—but no, neither of us can take the blame for the unavoidable.

We blame others—doctors, nurses, hospitals, emergency personnel, anyone who comes to mind—anyone who in any way could have contributed to our grief.

It's normal—and it passes. It only becomes a concern when that blame sinks deeper and deeper into the human spirit and resides there to take on the form of bitterness. It's then that help is needed to bring blame and bitterness into sharp focus.

There are sixteen "Why's" in the book of Job.

> Why was I born?[4]
> Why can't I die?[5]
> Why is God doing this to me?[6]
> Why doesn't God forgive me?[7]

Sixteen times Job asks, "Why?"

Sixteen times he hurls this question heavenward—and never gets a response.

When God does speak, He never addresses Job's questions.

He never describes the challenge thrown down by Satan, recorded in the early chapters.

He never explains the greater contest being run in full view of the spiritual world.

He never discusses the "high stakes" that have been laid on heaven's table as God had "put His money on Job" and won. He never explains "Why."

I have long since quit seeking the answer to that question in my own life. I really don't know why God does things the way He does, and I'm not sure that I'll ever know. I have a hunch that heaven is going to be so spectacular that I'll not even want to take time out then to seek the answers to so many of life's un-answerables.

God owes me no explanation. He has the right to do what He wants, when He wants, and how He wants. *Why?* Because He's God.

It's interesting to note in Job that, in response to sixteen "Why's," there are fifty-nine "Who's" in the book.

Martha's aunt visited us shortly after Jimmy's death and listened to our "Why's" until she found an appropriate moment. Then she said, "It might help if you changed the spelling of that word. Try spelling it with an 'o' instead of a 'y'. Change the word from 'Why' to 'Who'."

That's what God does in His speech to Job.

Job didn't need to know why these things happened as they did—he just needed to know Who was responsible and Who was in control. He just needed to know God.

When he said in chapter 42, verse 2, "I know that Thou canst do all things, and that no purpose of Thine can be thwarted," he was finally changing his "Why" to "Who."

He was finally letting God be God in his life.

If there is anything that we need during any of life's baffling or bewildering experiences, it is not an explanation, but just a fresh, new look at God.

Footnotes

Preface

1. Job 1:1
2. Text from PEANUTS by Charles M. Schulz; © 1967 United Feature Syndicate, Inc.

Chapter One

1. Job 2:7
2. Job 2:8
3. Job 2:8
4. Job 7:4
5. Job 7:5
6. Job 7:5
7. Job 3:24
8. Job 13:14
9. Job 13:28
10. Job 2:8
11. Job 16:16
12. Job 16:8
13. Job 16:7
14. Job 19:17
15. Job 9:18
16. Job 9:18
17. Job 19:20
18. Job 30:30
19. Job 30:30
20. Job 30:17
21. Job 16: 9, 10
22. Job 16:12
23. Job 16:13

Chapter Two

1. Job 29:7 TLB*
2. Job 29:12 TLB
3. Job 29:16 TLB
4. Job 29:14 TLB
5. Job 29:13 TLB
6. Job 29:17 TLB
7. Job 29:8 TLB
8. Job 29:21 TLB
9. Job 29:22 TLB
10. Job 29:11 TLB
11. Job 29:13 TLB
12. Job 29:15 TLB
13. Job 29:15 TLB
14. Job 29:16 TLB
15. Job 29:20 TLB
16. Job 29:24 TLB
17. Job 29:25 TLB
18. Job 1:8 TLB
19. Job 1:2, 3 TLB
20. Job 29:6 TLB
21. Job 1:4
22. Job 1:5 TLB
23. Job 29:4 TLB
24. Job 1:8
25. Job 29:18 TLB

*The Living Bible

Chapter Three

1. Job 1:18
2. Job 1:14-15
3. Job 1:16
4. Job 1:17
5. Job 1:18, 19
6. Job 1:20
7. Job 1:20-22
8. Job 1:22 TLB
9. Job 1:21
10. Job 2:10 TLB
11. Job 29:2 TLB
12. Job 29:2 TLB
13. Job 29:4 TLB
14. Job 29:5 TLB
15. Job 29:6 TLB
16. Job 29:8 TLB
17. Job 29:8 TLB
18. Job 29:9 TLB
19. Job 30:1 TLB
20. Job 30:9 TLB
21. Job 30:10 TLB
22. Job 30:13 TLB
23. Job 30:14 TLB
24. Job 30:15 TLB
25. Job 30:16 TLB
26. Job 30:20 TLB
27. Job 30:31 TLB
28. Job 19:17 TLB

Chapter Four

1. Job 2:11
2. Job 2:12
3. Job 2:13
4. Job 2:12
5. Job 2:13
6. Job 2:13
7. Job 3:1-23
8. Job 4:1-5 TLB
9. Job 8:2 TLB
10. Job 11:1, 2 TLB
11. Job 4:7 TLB
12. Job 8:6 TLB
13. Job 11:6 TLB
14. Job 6:10-30 TLB
15. Job 10:1-8 TLB
16. Job 22:5-9 TLB
17. Job 31:1-35 TLB

Chapter Five

1. Job 32:4-6
2. Job 32:2, 3
3. Job 32:19, 20
4. Job 33:12 TLB
5. Job 33:10
6. Job 33:13
7. Job 34:9 TLB
8. Job 34:35-37 TLB
9. Job 35:16 TLB

Chapter Six

1. Job 9:32-35
2. Job 36:3-6
3. Job 36:20 TLB
4. Job 36:26-28 TLB
5. Job 36:29 TLB
6. Job 36:29 TLB
7. Job 36:30-32 TLB
8. Job 36:33 TLB
9. Job 37:1-13 TLB
10. Job 37:22-24 TLB

Chapter Seven

1. Job 10:2 TLB
2. Job 10:18 TLB
3. Job 34:5 TLB
4. Genesis 3:8
5. Genesis 17:3
6. Exodus 3:6
7. Isaiah 6:5
8. Ezekiel 1:28
9. Daniel 8:18
10. Acts 9:3-9

Chapter Eight

1. Job 38:2 TLB
2. Job 38:4-40:2 TLB
3. Job 40:4-5 TLB
4. Job 40:7 TLB
5. Job 40:8, 9 TLB
6. Job 40:10-12 TLB
7. Job 40:15-24 TLB
8. Job 41:1-34 TLB
9. Job 41:10 TLB
10. Job 42:1-2 TLB
11. Job 42:3-6 TLB

Chapter Nine

1. Job 42:8, 9 TLB
2. Job 42:10, 11 TLB
3. Job 42:16 TLB
4. Job 42:17 TLB

Chapter Ten

1. Job 1:6
2. Job 1:7; 1 Peter 5:8
3. Job 1:8 TLB
4. Job 1:9-11 TLB
5. Job 1:12 TLB
6. Job 1:21
7. Job 1:22
8. Job 2:3 TLB
9. Job 2:4, 5 TLB
10. Job 2:6 TLB

Chapter Eleven

1. Job 1:11; 2:5
2. John 15:5
3. Luke 6:23
4. 2 Timothy 1:12

Chapter Twelve

1. Harold S. Kushner, *When Bad Things Happen to Good People* (New York: Avon Books, 1981), p. 30.
2. Ibid., p. 34.
3. Ibid., p. 43.
4. Ibid.
5. Ibid., p. 148.
6. Job 33:8-13
7. Job 33:12-13
8. Job 33:13-16
9. Psalm 139:7-10
10. Job 34:7-13
11. Job 42:2 TLB
12. John 19:10, 11
13. Luke 22:31

Chapter Thirteen

1. Job 42:7
2. Job 42:7, 8
3. Psalm 147:5
4. Isaiah 40:28
5. Romans 11:33
6. Isaiah 55:9

Chapter Fourteen

1. Don Baker and Emery Nester, *Depression: Finding Hope and Meaning in Life's Darkest Shadow* (Portland, Ore.: Multnomah Press, 1983).
2. Job 3:11-21 TLB
3. Job 3:13-22 TLB
4. Job 17:1, 16 TLB
5. Job 14:11, 12 TLB
6. Job 14:14 TLB
7. Job 19:26, 27 TLB
8. Job 36:20 TLB
9. Job 38:17 TLB
10. Hebrews 9:27

Chapter Fifteen

1. Job 7:11
2. Job 10:1
3. Job 38:2
4. Psalm 78:17-57
5. Exodus 3:17
6. Job 40:4 TLB
7. Job 42:2

Chapter Sixteen

1. Job 40:4 TLB
2. Job 42:2 TLB
3. Job 42:7 TLB
4. Job 42:8 TLB
5. Job 42:9 TLB
6. Job 42:10 TLB

Chapter Seventeen

1. John 11:21
2. John 11:32
3. John 11:25, 26
4. Job 3:11 TLB
5. Job 3:12 TLB
6. Job 7:20 TLB
7. Job 7:21 TLB

Bibliography

Archer, Gleason L., Jr. *The Book of Job: God's Answer to the Problem of Undeserved Suffering.* Grand Rapids: Baker Book House, 1982.

Barnes, Albert. *Notes on the Old Testament: Job, vols. 1 and 2.* Grand Rapids: Baker Book House, 1949.

Cambridge Bible for Schools and Colleges. *The Book of Job.* Cambridge: University Press, New ed., 1918.

Epp, Theodore H. *Why Do Christians Suffer?* Lincoln, Neb.: Back to the Bible, 1970.

McGee, J. Vernon. *Job.* Pasadena: Thru the Bible Books, 1981.

Scammon, John H. *If I Could Find God: Anguish and Faith in the Book of Job.* Valley Forge, Pa.: Judson Press, 1974.

Stedman, Ray C. *Expository Studies in Job: Behind Suffering.* Waco, Tex.: Word Books, 1981.

Zuck, Roy B. *Job.* Chicago: Moody Press, 1978.